God's Forgiveness to Man

Wazer H. Walker

God's Forgiveness to Man

Scripture quotations are taken from the King James Version (KJV) of the Bible.

This book is intended for educational and spiritual purposes. The views expressed in this work are those of the author and are based on the interpretation of Scripture. Readers are encouraged to study the Bible personally and seek spiritual guidance as needed.

Published independently.

First Edition, 2026

Printed in the United States of America

This book, God's Forgiveness to Man, is lovingly dedicated to my family, whose lives have been a constant reminder to me of both the need for grace and the beauty of it lived out.

To my beloved wife, Karen—your steadfast love, quiet strength, and enduring faith have been a continual testimony of God's kindness in my life. You have walked beside me through every season, offering encouragement, patience, and wisdom. Your life reflects the very grace this book seeks to proclaim.

To my son, Joel—may you grow to know deeply the richness of God's mercy and the power of His forgiveness. May your life be marked by truth, courage, and a heart that both receives and extends grace.

To my daughter, Ruth-Ann—your life is a gift, full of promise and light. May you always walk in the assurance that you are deeply loved by God, and may His forgiveness shape your identity and guide your steps.

Each of you has, in your own way, reminded me that forgiveness is not merely a doctrine to be studied, but a reality to be lived. This work is, in part, the fruit of your love and presence in my life.

With gratitude and love, I dedicate this book to you.

Foreword

Few themes in Scripture are as profound or as scandalous as the forgiveness of God. It stands at the very heart of the gospel—shining as both a deep mystery and humanity's greatest hope. In a world marked by estrangement and moral failure, the question is not whether forgiveness is needed, but whether it is truly possible. *God's Forgiveness to Man* answers that question with biblical fidelity and spiritual urgency.

Contemporary thought often reduces forgiveness to mere sentimentality or therapy. Yet, as this book reveals, divine forgiveness is never cheap. It is rooted in the character of a God who is both perfectly holy and immeasurably merciful. This work refuses to dilute the seriousness of sin while magnifying the glory of grace, leading the reader toward true restoration of the soul.

This is more than an intellectual exercise; it is a pastoral invitation to those carrying the heavy burden of shame. It calls us back to a vision of forgiveness that is robust, transformative, and anchored in revelation. As you turn these pages, you are invited to behold the magnitude of a mercy that overturns our natural sense of justice. May this work not only inform your mind but transform your heart.

Soli Deo Gloria.[1]

---

[1] *Soli Deo Gloria is a Latin phrase that means "Glory to God alone."*

Introduction:

Forgiveness stands at the very heart of the Christian faith. It is not merely a moral ideal or a secondary theme—it is the axis upon which the entire message of the gospel turns. Without forgiveness, the Christian message loses its meaning, its power, and its relevance. At its core, Christianity is the story of a broken relationship between humanity and God—and the divine initiative to restore it.

God's forgiveness is the cornerstone of this restoration. It is not simply the release from the bondage of sin, but an invitation into renewed relationship with the Creator. What was fractured in the beginning is made whole again through grace. In a world marked by division, guilt, and unrest, forgiveness stands as a beacon of hope, offering reconciliation, renewal, and the promise of eternal life. Through forgiveness, God reveals not only the depth of His mercy, but also the integrity of His justice and the richness of His love.

Throughout Scripture, forgiveness is not presented as optional, nor as an occasional act of divine kindness. It is central to God's redemptive plan. The Old Testament sacrificial system pointed toward the necessity of atonement, revealing that sin carried real consequence and required a remedy beyond human effort. The New Testament brings this reality into full clarity through the life, death, and resurrection of Jesus Christ. In Him, forgiveness is no longer anticipated—

it is accomplished. What was once foreshadowed becomes fulfilled, and what was once hoped for becomes reality.

Forgiveness, therefore, is not an abstract concept. It is a divine act rooted in God's character—His holiness, His justice, and His covenant love. While modern culture often reduces forgiveness to emotional release or personal closure, Scripture presents something far deeper. Forgiveness is not merely therapeutic; it is transformative. It does not simply ease the conscience—it restores the soul.

At the center of this need is the human condition itself. Humanity's deepest problem is not merely moral failure, but separation from God. From the fall onward, the human story has been marked by rebellion, guilt, and distance from the One who created us. This separation cannot be resolved through effort, discipline, or self-improvement. It requires intervention. It requires grace.

This reality has been recognized throughout the history of Christian thought. The human heart, restless and searching, cannot find peace apart from God. Forgiveness, therefore, is not just a theological idea—it is the answer to a deeply human need. And yet, in the modern world, forgiveness often feels difficult to understand. In a culture that demands justice yet struggles to accept grace, forgiveness can appear unjust, even offensive. How can wrongdoing be pardoned without consequence? How can a holy God forgive without compromising righteousness?

The answer is found at the center of the gospel. At the cross of Jesus Christ, justice and mercy meet. Sin is not ignored—it is addressed. Justice is not denied—it is fulfilled. And mercy is not withheld—it is extended. In Christ, God demonstrates that He is both just and the One who justifies. The cross reveals that forgiveness is neither cheap nor careless—it is costly, intentional, and complete.

This book explores the doctrine of forgiveness from biblical, theological, and pastoral perspectives. It traces its foundation in Scripture, its fulfillment in Christ, and its transformative power in the life of the believer. It examines not only what forgiveness is, but what it does—how it restores identity, heals relationships, and reshapes the way we live.

Ultimately, this work seeks to present forgiveness not merely as a doctrine to be understood, but as a reality to be experienced. Because forgiveness is not just part of the Christian message—
it is its very heart.

1: The Problem — Sin & Separation

There are truths that humanity has wrestled with across generations—truths that are not easily dismissed, yet not always readily embraced. Among them is the reality of sin. In an age that often celebrates self-definition and autonomy, the suggestion that something is fundamentally disordered within the human condition can feel both uncomfortable and unwelcome.

And yet, beneath the surface of human experience, there remains a persistent awareness that something is not as it should be. This awareness does not always take the form of theological language; rather, it is often encountered in quiet moments—when distractions fade, when reflection becomes unavoidable, and when one is faced with the undeniable tension between who they are and who they know they ought to be.

The Internal Tension

This internal tension reveals itself in ways both subtle and unmistakable. It appears in the gap between intention and action—in the desire to do what is right and the repeated failure to follow through. It surfaces in relationships, where love is often mixed with selfishness, and where trust is easily broken but difficult to restore. It is present in the recurring patterns of thought and behavior that resist even our most sincere attempts to change.

Over time, it becomes clear that this is not an occasional flaw, but something deeper—something woven into the fabric of human experience.

This brokenness is not confined to the individual; it is reflected across the entire human story. It can be seen in cycles of injustice, in the persistence of conflict, in the misuse of power, and in the ways people wound one another, both intentionally and unintentionally. Despite progress in knowledge, culture, and innovation, the same underlying issues remain.

Humanity continues to advance outwardly while struggling inwardly. The problem has never been merely external—it is internal.

The Nature of the Condition

Scripture identifies this condition with clarity: it is sin. Sin is not merely a collection of isolated wrong acts, nor is it limited to outward behavior. It is a condition that affects the entirety of human nature—shaping desires, distorting perception, and influencing the will.

It is the inward inclination away from God and toward self. It is not only what we do when we choose wrongly; it is the deeper reality that inclines us to make those choices in the first place.

At its core, sin produces separation. Humanity was created for communion with God—marked by closeness, trust, and unhindered fellowship. There was no distance, no fear, no barrier. The relationship between Creator and creation was whole.

But that relationship was disrupted. What was once characterized by intimacy became marked by distance. Sin introduced not only disobedience, but estrangement. And this estrangement is not merely symbolic—it is relational and spiritual in its deepest sense.

The Resulting Unrest

It manifests as guilt, as shame, and as a subtle yet profound disconnection from the presence of God. It creates an internal unrest that cannot be fully explained or easily resolved. In place of clarity, there is confusion. In place of peace, there is striving.

Humanity continues to search—for meaning, for identity, for fulfillment—yet often does so apart from the very source in which those things are found. This is why even the most fulfilled lives can still feel incomplete. There is a longing that remains—a quiet awareness that what we were made for has not yet been fully experienced.

This separation extends beyond the relationship between humanity and God. It affects how individuals understand themselves, often producing a tension between pride and insecurity, self-justification and self-condemnation.

At times, people elevate themselves, seeking to prove worth and establish identity through achievement or comparison. At other times, they are weighed down by inadequacy, unable to escape the awareness of their own failure. Both extremes reveal the same underlying issue—a fractured understanding of self rooted in separation from God.

The Fractured Existence

It also affects relationships with others. The same humanity capable of deep love is also capable of deep harm. Trust is built, but it is also broken. Unity is desired, yet division persists. Even in the closest relationships, there is often a tension—a reminder that something is not fully aligned. The result is a fractured existence in which glimpses of goodness remain, yet are consistently undermined by the deeper reality of brokenness. Throughout history, humanity has attempted to address this condition in various ways:

- **Moral Improvement:** Believing that better behavior will resolve the problem.
- **Philosophy:** Seeking answers through reason and reflection.

- **Success:** Hoping that achievement will quiet the unrest.
- **Distraction:** Filling lives with activity to avoid confronting deeper questions.

While these approaches may produce temporary relief or outward change, they do not reach the root of the issue. Because the problem of sin is not merely behavioral—it is ontological. It is not simply what humanity does; it is what humanity has become.

The Need for Restoration

And because of this, the gap created by sin cannot be bridged through human effort alone. The distance is too great, and the condition too pervasive. No amount of self-correction can fully restore what has been fundamentally disrupted. The more humanity strives to fix itself, the more it becomes aware of its limitations.

The effort itself reveals the depth of the problem.

This is what makes the reality of sin so profound. It exposes both the brokenness of humanity and the inability of humanity to repair that brokenness on its own. And yet, even within this condition, there remains something significant—an awareness that things are not as they should be.

It points to a deeper truth: humanity was made for more than its current condition. We were not created for separation or unrest. We were created for relationship.

Understanding the depth of this problem is essential, not as a means of condemnation, but as a foundation for clarity. If sin were trivial, its consequences would be minimal. If separation were superficial, it could be easily repaired. But the reality presented in Scripture is far more serious.

Humanity does not need mere improvement—it needs restoration. And restoration cannot originate from within the problem itself. If reconciliation is to occur, it must come from the One from whom humanity has been separated. It must come from God.

2: The Nature of God's Forgiveness

God's forgiveness is not merely the overlooking of sin, nor is it a passive decision to ignore wrongdoing. It is a deliberate and active movement toward reconciliation—a divine initiative in which God restores humanity to Himself.

Forgiveness, in its truest sense, does not minimize the gravity of sin; rather, it fully acknowledges it. It recognizes the weight of human rebellion and responds not by dismissing it, but by addressing it in a way that makes restoration possible.

In this way, forgiveness is not a compromise of God's holiness, but an expression of it.

It is an act of profound grace in which God chooses to bear the cost of what humanity could not repair, offering release and renewal in a manner fully consistent with His character.

A Relational Restoration

At its core, forgiveness is relational rather than transactional. It is not a mere exchange or a legal adjustment; it is the restoration of a broken relationship. Humanity was created for fellowship with God, and sin disrupted that fellowship.

Forgiveness, therefore, is not simply about removing guilt—it is about restoring connection. It flows not from human effort or merit, but from the very nature of God Himself.

Scripture consistently reveals God as merciful and gracious, slow to anger, and abounding in steadfast love. Forgiveness is not something God does reluctantly; it is something that flows naturally from who He is.

The Harmony of Attributes

The forgiveness offered by God is an outpouring of His righteousness, justice, and love. These attributes are not in conflict with one another, but are perfectly united within Him.

God does not forgive by setting aside justice, nor does He uphold justice at the expense of mercy. Instead, His forgiveness reflects a harmony of both. He remains just, even as He justifies. He remains holy, even as He draws near to the sinner.

This reveals something deeply personal about the nature of God. He is not distant or indifferent. He is not a detached judge issuing decrees from afar. He is a compassionate Father who understands human frailty and desires restoration for His children.

His forgiveness is not cold or mechanical—it is relational, intentional, and filled with purpose.

Holiness and Mercy

Forgiveness begins with the character of God. Scripture repeatedly presents Him as both holy and merciful, and these qualities are never portrayed as contradictory. His holiness means that He is completely pure and set apart from sin, while His mercy reveals His willingness to engage with humanity despite its brokenness. Together, these attributes form the foundation of divine forgiveness.

It is because God is holy that sin must be addressed, and it is because He is merciful that sinners are not abandoned. In Him, justice and compassion are not opposing forces, but perfectly aligned realities.

The Depth of the Language

The language of Scripture further deepens this understanding. In the Hebrew tradition, specific words are used to describe forgiveness in ways that reveal its depth and significance.

- **Divine Forgiveness:** One term refers specifically to divine forgiveness, emphasizing that true forgiveness ultimately belongs to God alone.
- **Atonement:** Another term conveys the idea of covering or atoning, pointing to the necessity of dealing with sin in a way that removes its barrier.

These words reflect a truth that runs throughout Scripture: forgiveness is not merely emotional, nor is it superficial. It is covenantal, sacrificial, and rooted in the very structure of God's relationship with His people.

The Source of Restoration

This understanding has been affirmed throughout the history of Christian thought. Theologians have long recognized that forgiveness cannot originate from human effort. Humanity does not possess the ability to cleanse itself from sin or restore what has been broken.

Forgiveness, therefore, must come from God. It is an act of divine love, extended not because it is earned, but because it is given. It is grounded not in human goodness, but in divine grace.

This reveals the true nature of God's forgiveness. It is not conditional upon human perfection, nor is it dependent on human ability. It is initiated by God, sustained by His character, and completed through His action.

It reaches into the deepest areas of human brokenness and offers something that cannot be achieved by any other means—restoration.

3: Forgiveness, Justice, and Holiness

If forgiveness is real, then a deeper question must be asked: How can a holy and just God forgive at all?.

This question is not merely philosophical—it is central to understanding the nature of God. If God is truly holy, then He cannot tolerate sin. If He is truly just, then He cannot ignore it. And yet, throughout Scripture, He is revealed as One who forgives.

At first glance, these truths appear to stand in tension with one another. Human experience often reinforces this tension, as in our world, justice and mercy are frequently seen as opposites. To show mercy can feel like weakening justice, while to enforce justice can seem like withholding compassion.

The Cost of Divine Forgiveness

Forgiveness, in many cases, is misunderstood as overlooking wrongdoing or excusing what has been done. But divine forgiveness is not like human forgiveness. God does not forgive by dismissing sin—He forgives by dealing with it fully. His holiness does not diminish in the presence of mercy, and His justice is not suspended in order to show compassion. Instead, both are upheld perfectly.

God's holiness means that sin is taken seriously. It is not minimized, rationalized, or redefined.

His justice means that sin carries consequence. It cannot simply be set aside, because to do so would contradict His own character. This is what makes forgiveness so profound: it is not a denial of justice, but its fulfillment.

The Necessity of Sacrifice

True forgiveness is always costly. Whenever a wrong is committed, someone must bear the weight of it. In human relationships, this cost is often absorbed quietly through patience or restraint.

But on a divine level, the cost of sin is far greater. It is not merely emotional or relational—it is moral and spiritual, carrying consequences that extend beyond what humanity can resolve on its own. This is why forgiveness cannot be understood apart from sacrifice.

Scripture makes clear that forgiveness is not achieved through intention or effort alone. It is not brought about by simply deciding to let something go. Rather, it is secured through the bearing of consequence.

Fulfillment in Christ

In the Christian faith, this is accomplished through Christ. God does not ignore sin—He confronts it. He does not set justice aside—He fulfills it.

But instead of requiring humanity to bear the full weight of its own wrongdoing, He provides a substitute. Christ becomes the one who carries what humanity could not. This is where the depth of divine wisdom is revealed:

- **Justice is upheld:** Because sin is judged.
- **Mercy is extended:** Because the sinner is spared.

The Revelation of the Cross

The cross stands at the center of this reality. It is not merely a moment of suffering, but a revelation. It reveals the seriousness of sin because it required such a cost. It reveals the justice of God because that cost was not avoided. And it reveals the love of God because He Himself provided the means to bear it.

Here, holiness, justice, and mercy are not in conflict, but in perfect harmony. This challenges the way forgiveness is often understood as something casual or superficial. It is a deeply costly act rooted in truth, righteousness, and love.

Far from diminishing the seriousness of sin, forgiveness magnifies it. It shows that sin is so significant that it could not be ignored. At the same time, it reveals that God's love is even greater—that He was willing to provide a way for restoration without compromising His own nature.

4: Biblical Foundations of Forgiveness

The concept of divine forgiveness is not introduced abruptly in Scripture; it is developed progressively, woven throughout the biblical narrative from beginning to end.

The Old Testament lays a profound theological foundation for understanding what forgiveness is, why it is necessary, and how it is ultimately made possible. From the earliest pages of Scripture, it becomes clear that forgiveness is not incidental to God's plan—it is central to it.

The Old Testament Framework

Within the Old Testament, the sacrificial system established under the Mosaic Covenant serves as one of the clearest frameworks for understanding forgiveness. These sacrifices were not arbitrary rituals, but were given by God as a means of addressing sin .

The shedding of blood pointed to a sobering truth: *sin is costly*. It cannot simply be ignored; it must be dealt with in a way that satisfies justice.

- **Atonement:** The life of the flesh is in the blood, given for the purpose of making atonement.

- **Substitution:** Forgiveness required more than intention; it required something to stand in the place of the sinner and bear the weight of what had been done.
- **The Heart:** External ritual alone was never the goal; God desired repentance, humility, and a genuine turning toward Him.

"Though your sins are like scarlet, they shall be as white as snow,"

Fulfillment in the New Testament

With the arrival of Jesus, the concept of forgiveness is brought into sharp and transformative focus. What was once anticipated is now revealed; what was once symbolized is now embodied.

In His teaching, His actions, and ultimately His mission, Jesus makes clear that forgiveness is central to the Kingdom of God. In the Lord's Prayer, He teaches that forgiveness is both a gift to be received and a responsibility to be lived out.

Through His parables, Jesus further illustrates the nature of divine forgiveness:

- **Eagerness:** In the story of the Prodigal Son, forgiveness is not reluctant but eager, compassionate, and immediate.

- **Restoration:** The father does not wait for perfection; he responds to repentance with restoration.
- **A Continual Posture:** Forgiveness is not an occasional act for the follower of Christ, but a defining characteristic of their life.

The Proclamation of the Early Church

Following the resurrection, forgiveness becomes the central proclamation of the gospel itself. At Pentecost, the call was clear: repent and be baptized for the forgiveness of sins.

The apostolic writings further emphasize that forgiveness is an ongoing reality. Believers are called to live in continual awareness of God's mercy, returning to Him in confession and receiving cleansing again and again. This relationship is sustained through:

- **Honesty**
- **Humility**
- **Dependence on Grace**

In this way, forgiveness becomes the lifeblood of the Christian life—it is what initiates restoration, and it is what sustains it .

5: The Weight of Sin

Scripture does not speak of sin lightly. From the earliest pages of the biblical story, sin is presented not as a minor misstep, but as a rupture—something that disturbs what was meant to be whole.

The sacrificial system, the language of atonement, and the repeated call to repentance all point to a reality that cannot be ignored: *sin carries weight*. This is not just moral weight, but relational and spiritual weight. It is a force that disrupts, distorts, and separates.

The Accumulation of Brokenness

What begins as disobedience does not remain isolated—it spreads, shaping thoughts, desires, and patterns over time. This weight is often carried quietly. It shows up in several ways:

- **Internal Guilt:** Lingering longer than expected.
- **Deep Shame:** Settling deeper than words can reach.
- **Quiet Fear:** The persistent anxiety of being fully known.
- **The Inability to Rest:** A constant, underlying need to "prove" oneself.

The weight of sin is not only internal—it is relational. It is the turning away from the One for whom we were created.

The Rupture of Relationship

Sin is not just the breaking of a rule; it is the breaking of a relationship. There is no relationship greater than that between humanity and God, which is why the weight of its rupture is so significant. Throughout history, humanity has attempted to manage this weight in different ways:

- **Ignorance:** Convincing ourselves it isn't serious.
- **Compensation:** Hoping good choices will outweigh the bad.
- **Internalization:** Carrying the guilt inwardly without a path to freedom.

None of these approaches remove the weight; they only mask it. Sin does not dissolve with time or disappear through distraction.

A Burden Beyond Human Strength

The sacrificial system revealed that something had to be given in order for sin to be addressed; it taught that sin carries a cost that must be paid. Yet even those sacrifices pointed beyond themselves. They exposed the problem, but they did not fully resolve it.

They pointed forward to a moment when the weight of sin would not merely be acknowledged but lifted.

The Central Tension:

1. Sin demands justice.

2. Separation demands restoration.
3. Humanity stands in the middle, unable to resolve either.

The weight of sin is not meant to crush, but to reveal—not to condemn, but to clarify. It shows us what we cannot fix and what we cannot carry. It points us to the reality that someone greater is needed.

If the burden is heavy, then the one who removes it must be stronger.

6: The Cost — The Cross

At the center of the Christian faith stands the cross. It is not a decoration or a mere tradition, but the place where everything was decided. It is here that forgiveness is no longer an idea, but an accomplished reality.

Throughout Scripture, the question was raised: *How can a holy and just God forgive sinful humanity?* At the cross, that question is answered once and for all—not with words, but with sacrifice.

The Necessity of the Price

Forgiveness is never detached from cost. From the beginning, God made it clear that sin was not something to be dismissed or explained away.

The shedding of blood in the Old Testament was a message and a shadow of something greater to come. It declared that sin demands a price, and that price cannot be ignored. The death of Jesus was not an accident of history; it was the only way reconciliation could be achieved without compromising the very nature of God.

"God does not forgive by ignoring sin. He forgives by confronting it. Fully. Completely. Without compromise."

The Exposure of Sin

At the cross, sin is not minimized—it is exposed. Every act of rebellion and every hidden failure is brought into the light. The full weight of it falls not on humanity, but on Christ. He bears it all.

- **The Judgment:** Justice is not removed; it is executed.
- **The Consequence:** Not erased but absorbed.
- **The Penalty:** Not avoided but paid in full.

This reveals a staggering truth: Sin is more serious than we imagine, and God's love is greater than we can comprehend.

Where Justice and Mercy Meet

Theologians have wrestled with this for centuries, yet the truth remains: at the cross, justice and mercy do not compete. They meet perfectly and completely.

Justice is upheld because sin is judged.

Mercy is extended because the sinner is spared.

God does not stand at a distance demanding payment—He steps forward and pays it Himself.

The Language of Freedom

Scripture describes this forgiveness as release—a setting free from what once bound us. It is liberation from guilt and condemnation.

However, this freedom is not cheap; it is purchased with blood. Another word used in Scripture speaks to satisfaction—the idea that what justice required has been fully met.

Nothing remains unpaid.

Nothing remains outstanding.

The work is complete.

The Turning Point

The cross stands as the foundation of forgiveness and the only place where the problem of sin is truly resolved. It is the very place where death seems to win, yet life is made possible.

The cross is not only where sin is dealt with; it is where redemption begins. Through the cross, forgiveness becomes more than a promise—it becomes our reality.

7: The Depth of God's Love

The cross is not only a demonstration of divine justice—it is the clearest and most profound revelation of God's love. What was accomplished there was not merely the resolution of a legal problem, but the expression of a deeply personal and sacrificial love that reaches beyond human comprehension.

In the suffering and death of Christ, love is not simply spoken—it is displayed, embodied, and proven. Jesus Himself declared that there is no greater love than this: that someone would lay down his life for his friends.

A Love That Enters In

These are not abstract words; they find their fullest meaning at the cross. There, Christ does not love from a distance:

- **He enters into human suffering.**
- **He endures betrayal, rejection, and pain.**
- **He willingly gives Himself**, not out of obligation, but out of love.

The sacrifice of Christ demonstrates the value God places on humanity. It shows that we are not overlooked, forgotten, or without worth. God did not withhold what was most precious to Him; He gave freely, fully, and without reservation.

Beyond Worthiness

The cross is the outworking of divine compassion—a love that moves toward humanity in its brokenness rather than away from it.

"God does not wait for humanity to become worthy of love; He demonstrates His love in the very midst of its unworthiness."

This transforms the meaning of forgiveness. It is not simply the cancellation of a debt, but the restoration of a relationship. Through Christ, God does not merely pardon—He draws near, He embraces, and He restores.

From Pardon to Relationship

Those who receive forgiveness are not simply declared innocent; they are brought into something greater.

- **They are welcomed into relationship.**
- **They are no longer defined by what they have done**, but by what has been done for them.
- **They are not treated as outsiders**, but embraced as children.

This is the depth of God's love: a love that gives, sacrifices, and restores . It is a love that does not remain distant but comes near, meeting brokenness with grace.

The Confirmation of Victory

The cross is where forgiveness was secured, but the resurrection is where it was confirmed. Without the resurrection, the death of Jesus would remain a powerful moment of sacrifice, but not one of victory.

The resurrection declares that the work was sufficient and accepted. It is the unmistakable confirmation that sin has been fully dealt with, justice has been satisfied, and death itself has been overcome.

A Love That Measures Worth

The sacrifice of Christ is the ultimate metric of human value. It reveals a truth that is both humbling and astonishing: the depth of God's love is measured not by what He says, but by what He was willing to give. And what He gave was everything.

In a world that constantly assigns value based on performance, status, or utility, the cross speaks a different language. It declares that:

- **You are not overlooked:** God sees the individual in the midst of the crowd.
- **You are not forgotten:** The divine initiative was taken specifically to find the lost.
- **You are not without worth:** The price paid—the life of the Son—reflects the value the Father places on the relationship.

The Personal Invitation

This love is not a generalized sentiment directed at a nameless crowd; it is intensely personal. It speaks to the deepest places of human need—the longing to be known, to be accepted, and to be restored. Because this love is personal, it is also specific. It reaches:

- **Beyond failure:** It does not turn away when we stumble.
- **Past mistakes:** It is not hindered by our history.
- **Through shame and guilt:** It moves directly toward the places we try to hide.

The Divine Embrace

The result of this love is a radical change in standing. Because of what was accomplished at the cross, those who receive forgiveness are no longer outsiders or orphans. They are drawn into a new family dynamic:

"They are not merely pardoned—they are received. They are not kept at a distance—they are drawn near. They are not treated as outsiders—they are embraced as children."

This is the transformative power of the Depth of God's Love. It does not merely address the problem of sin; it transforms the sinner from a defendant into a beloved child. It is a love that does not remain distant but comes near, anchoring our identity in the grace that has already been given.

8: The Resurrection – The Seal

The cross is where forgiveness was secured; the resurrection is where it was confirmed. Without the resurrection, the death of Jesus would remain a powerful moment of sacrifice and love, but it would ultimately be incomplete. It would stand as a tragedy, but not as a victory.

The resurrection transforms the meaning of the cross. It is the divine affirmation that the work of Christ was sufficient, that nothing more was required, and that nothing remained undone.

A Divine Declaration

When Jesus was raised from the dead, it was more than a miracle—it was a declaration. It was the unmistakable confirmation that:

- **Sin has been fully dealt with.**
- **Justice has been satisfied.**
- **Death itself has been overcome.**

What appeared to be defeat was revealed to be triumph. The grave, which had long stood as the ultimate symbol of human limitation, was entered—and then emptied.

The Proof of Forgiveness

Scripture declares that Jesus was "raised for our justification". This means the resurrection is inseparably tied to forgiveness. It is the moment where forgiveness moves from a promise to a proof, and from hope to certainty.

"Because of the resurrection, forgiveness is not uncertain—it is secure. It is not fragile—it is established."

It does not depend on human strength, consistency, or feeling. It rests on something unchanging and already completed outside of ourselves.

New Life and Transformation

The resurrection does more than confirm the past; it introduces what is now possible. Forgiveness is not merely the cancellation of guilt, but the beginning of new life. The same power that raised Christ from the dead becomes the foundation for transformation within the believer. It works to:

- Reshape desires.
- Renew the mind.
- Restore what was once broken.

The Eternal Guarantee

Through the resurrection, the past no longer has the power to define the future. What once seemed permanent has been undone.

The empty tomb stands as the guarantee that what God has begun, He will complete. It declares that forgiveness is not temporary, but enduring; not fragile, but unshakable; and secured forever.

The Vindication of Christ's Identity

The resurrection is not merely a post-script to the cross; it is the ultimate vindication of everything Jesus claimed to be. His authority was never confined to the words He spoke or the miracles He performed during His earthly ministry.

By rising from the grave, Jesus demonstrated that His authority reached into the very realm of death itself. It confirms that He is exactly who He said He is: the Son of God and the Savior of the world. Without this triumph, the cross would be the tragic end of a good man; with it, the cross is the glorious victory of a Risen King.

The End of the Final Enemy

In rising from the grave, Jesus demonstrates that nothing remains unconquered—not sin, not judgment, and not even death. The final enemy has been faced and defeated once and for all.

- **The Power of Death is Broken:** The grave is no longer the final word.
- **The Fear of the Grave is Removed:** What was once humanity's greatest fear has become the testimony of God's greatest victory.

- **A New Reality is Established:** The story of humanity no longer ends in loss, but in life.

Certainty Beyond Feeling

Perhaps the most practical aspect of the resurrection is the stability it brings to the believer's heart. Forgiveness often feels fragile because our emotions are fragile. We may feel forgiven one day and condemned the next. However, the resurrection anchors our hope in a historical fact rather than a fluctuating feeling.

- **It Silences Doubt:** Not by removing every question, but by establishing an unshakable foundation.
- **It Provides Constant Assurance:** Because He lives, the past no longer has authority over the present.
- **It Guarantees Completion:** The empty tomb is the proof that the debt has been paid in full and nothing remains unresolved.

"The resurrection is the moment where forgiveness moves from promise to proof, from hope to certainty."

An Invitation to Newness

Finally, the resurrection introduces a present reality: the same power that raised Christ is now working within the believer. It is not a distant historical power, but a present one that reshapes desires and restores what was broken.

It invites the believer into a life no longer defined by the gravity of their sin, but by the power of His grace. We are called not only to believe in what happened, but to live in the light of it every single day.

9: Why Grace Feel Unfair

There is something about grace that unsettles us. At first, it appears beautiful—the idea that forgiveness is offered freely and the weight of sin can be lifted feels like good news. And yet, for many, that same message begins to raise honest, difficult questions:

- **Is it really that simple?**
- **Is it fair?**
- **Why should someone who has done wrong receive the same forgiveness as someone who has tried to do right?**

These questions reveal a tension within the human heart between justice and mercy. We instinctively understand that wrong should be addressed and that actions should carry consequences.

The System of Exchange

The reason grace feels disruptive is that it challenges our sense of balance. The world is built on a system of exchange: effort is rewarded, and failure carries a consequence.

Grace does not follow this pattern. It gives where nothing has been earned, restores where nothing has been deserved, and offers what cannot be repaid. This discomfort begins because if grace is truly grace, it cannot be controlled, calculated, or limited to those who seem "worthy".

Redirected Justice

Grace feels unfair when we think forgiveness comes without cost. But forgiveness is not free—it is simply a cost that *we* did not pay.

At the cross, justice was not dismissed; it was fulfilled. The consequence was not removed; it was absorbed by Christ. What feels unfair to us is not that justice is absent, but that we are no longer required to bear it.

"Grace is not the absence of justice, but the redirection of it; not the denial of consequence, but the fulfillment of it in Christ."

The Barrier of Pride

Accepting grace requires us to let go of something deeply ingrained: the belief that we must earn what we receive. It confronts the idea that we can make ourselves right and asks us to *receive* rather than *achieve*.

There is also a second layer to this tension: grace feels unfair when applied to others. It is one thing to receive mercy for ourselves, but it is another to see it extended to someone who has caused harm—someone who, in our eyes, does not deserve it.

Better Than Fair

Grace reaches where we would not and gives where we would withhold. It exposes the condition of our own hearts and reminds us that if grace were based on worthiness, none would receive it.

- **Fairness** would give us what we deserve.
- **Grace** gives us what we could never deserve.

Once grace is embraced, the question changes from *"Is this fair?"* to *"How could this be given to me?"*. In that shift, pride softens, and gratitude begins to rise. Grace transforms our perspective, allowing us to see others not as people to measure, but as people in need of the same mercy we have been given.

10: Receiving Forgiveness

Forgiveness as revealed throughout Scripture, is not something humanity earns—it is something God gives.

Yet while it is freely offered, it is not passively received. It calls for a response. Divine forgiveness invites participation, not performance. It is extended by grace, but it must be received through a willing and responsive heart.

The Two Essential Movements

This response is consistently described in Scripture through two deeply connected realities: *Repentance* and *Faith*.

1. Repentance: The Decisive Turn

Repentance is more than a feeling. It is more than regret, more than guilt, and more than a moment of emotional awareness. It is a turning—a decisive shift of direction in both heart and life.

- **Seeing Clearly:** It involves recognizing sin for what it is—not excusing or minimizing it—and choosing to turn away.
- **Moving Toward God:** It is a movement away from self and toward the Creator.
- **The Divine Spark:** This turning is not rooted in human strength; it begins with the work of God within the heart to bring conviction and reveal truth.

2. Faith: The Posture of Trust

Faith is the personal entrusting of one's life to Christ. It is more than intellectual agreement; it is the decision to rely entirely on what has already been accomplished through Him.

- **Sufficiency:** To have faith is to believe that the work of the cross is enough.
- **Availability:** It is the belief that forgiveness is real and available because of divine grace, not personal worthiness.

"Repentance turns the heart away from sin; faith turns it toward Christ. One releases what cannot save; the other embraces the One who does."

A Transformation, Not a Transaction

Together, repentance and faith form the threshold through which forgiveness is received. This is not a transaction—it is a transformation. It is important to note that forgiveness is not granted because our repentance is perfect or our faith is strong; it is grounded entirely in the work of Christ. This truth brings:

- **Humility:** We are reminded that we cannot save ourselves.
- **Freedom:** We are assured that we do not have to.

The Ongoing Reality

Receiving forgiveness is not merely a one-time moment. While there is a beginning, there is also an ongoing reality marked by a continual dependence on God's grace. Just as any healthy relationship requires open communication, the life of faith involves a continual turning of the heart and a daily receiving of what has already been given.

In this way, forgiveness becomes something that is lived. It reshapes identity and reorients the heart. The one who receives it is no longer defined by failure, but by grace.

11: Why It's Hard to Receive Forgiveness

Receiving forgiveness should feel like relief, and yet for many, it does not. There is often a quiet resistance—subtle, persistent, and difficult to explain. While the mind may understand that the work of Christ is sufficient, the heart often hesitates, pulls back, and struggles to fully accept what is freely given.

The Lingering Shadows: Guilt vs. Shame

The difficulty often begins with a misunderstanding of our own internal pain. We must distinguish between the weight of our actions and the weight of our identity:

- **The Grip of Guilt:** This is the kind of regret that lingers and replays moments long after they have passed. It whispers that something is still owed or unresolved, even after forgiveness is declared.
- **The Burden of Shame:** While guilt says, *"I did something wrong,"* shame says, *"There is something wrong with me"*.
- **The Identity Shift:** Shame attaches itself to identity rather than actions. It convinces us that our past defines who we are, making grace feel "hard to believe".

The Habit of Earning

We are deeply conditioned by systems where effort leads to reward and failure requires compensation. This "performance mindset" is a major barrier to receiving divine mercy:

- **Self-Correction:** we often try to fix what we broke to prove we are worthy of being forgiven.
- **The Loss of Control:** Receiving forgiveness requires letting go of the illusion of self-reliance.
- **Trusting the Sufficiency:** It means trusting that Christ's work is enough, even when we feel it "shouldn't be".

The Fear of Being Known

Another significant barrier is the fear of total exposure. True forgiveness requires bringing hidden things into the light. We fear that if everything were truly seen, the offer of forgiveness would be withdrawn.

"Forgiveness is not given because something is hidden; it is given despite what is revealed."

There is no failure that surprises God, and no thought He has not already accounted for. He offers forgiveness fully and without condition.

The Process of Embracing

Receiving forgiveness is not always instantaneous; it is often a process of returning to the truth again and again. It involves choosing to believe God's word over our own feelings.

As this truth is embraced, the results are transformative:

- **The Removal of Condemnation:** Forgiveness does not erase memory, but it removes the authority of the past.
- **The Gift of Peace:** The soul begins to rest, not because the past is forgotten, but because it is finally forgiven.
- **True Freedom:** For those willing to let go of what they have been carrying, there is freedom waiting on the other side.

The Illusion of Self-Atonement

For many, the hardest part of receiving forgiveness is the subconscious belief that we must suffer in proportion to our failure. We often engage in "self-atonement," where we believe that by staying miserable, carrying a heavy countenance, or denying ourselves peace, we are somehow paying back the debt of our sin.

However, this mindset is a subtle rejection of the Cross. It suggests that Christ's sacrifice was a good start, but our personal suffering is what finally "settles the score".

- **The Trap of Penance:** We mistake self-punishment for piety.
- **The Rejection of the Gift:** By trying to pay for what has already been purchased, we miss the freedom of the gift.
- **The Weight of Performance:** We live as though our standing with God is a "probationary" status that we must maintain through perfect behavior.

The Distorted Image of the Father

Often, the struggle to receive forgiveness is rooted in a distorted view of God's character. If we view God as a distant, cold judge waiting for us to slip up, grace will always feel like a "trick" or a temporary reprieve rather than a permanent state of being.

- **Projecting Human Limits:** We project our own inability to truly let go of a grudge onto God.
- **The Expectation of Rejection:** We live in a defensive posture, waiting for the "other shoe to drop".
- **The Truth of the Gospel:** We must replace these projections with the biblical reality: God is not surprised by our failures, and His invitation is not based on our potential, but on His finished work.

"Forgiveness does not leave room for shame to define identity. If the record has been cleared, then the labels attached to it no longer hold authority."

Stepping Into the Light

The final barrier is the comfort of the dark. As strange as it sounds, shame can become a "comfortable" hiding place because it requires nothing of us but isolation. To receive forgiveness is to step into the light, which requires a radical honesty that can be terrifying.

- **Releasing the Crutch:** We must let go of the identity of "the failure" or "the victim of our own past".
- **Embracing the New:** We must accept a new identity that we didn't build and can't take credit for.
- **The Choice of Peace:** We must intentionally choose to believe what God says about us, even when it contradicts our internal monologue.

12: Gratitude & Worship

The experience of being forgiven does not leave a person unchanged. It awakens something deep within the heart, shifting what was once heavy to a state of lightness. When forgiveness is truly received, gratitude begins to rise—not as a rehearsed or forced obligation, but as a real, inevitable response to what has been given.

The Inevitability of Gratitude

Forgiveness naturally produces gratitude because it brings clarity to what has been removed. It is only when a person understands the weight of the guilt and the depth of the shame that was once carried that they can truly appreciate the mercy they have received.

This gratitude is not limited to a fleeting emotion; it transforms the way a person moves through the world. It becomes visible in:

- **Posture:** A shift from being burdened to being free.
- **Perspective:** Seeing the world through the lens of grace.
- **Response:** Living out a life that reflects the mercy received.

The Pattern of Worship

Scripture provides a powerful image of this response in the account of the woman who approached Jesus with perfume.

Aware of her past and the mercy she had been shown, her actions were unguarded and expressive. She poured out what she had because she could not hold it back; her gratitude became her worship.

"When mercy is understood, devotion follows."

Worship, therefore, is not limited to a specific place, a musical style, or a Sunday gathering. It is a way of living—a continual response to the goodness of God. It is reflected in:

- **Obedience:** Driven by thankfulness rather than obligation.
- **Surrender:** A willing and internal shift of the heart.
- **Service:** Loving others as a response to being loved.

A Life Reoriented

Forgiveness initiates a new way of living marked by awareness and devotion. The life of the believer is no longer centered on the self but is oriented around the One who forgives.

This gratitude is not shallow; it matures and strengthens over time. The more a person understands the weight of what has been forgiven, the deeper their worship becomes. It anchors the heart in something steady and unchanging.

In this way, worship becomes more than just an act—it becomes a life. The heart that has been forgiven cannot remain indifferent; it is drawn toward the One who forgives, again and again.

13: Forgiving Others

Forgiveness, once received, does not remain contained. It moves. It extends outward, reshaping not only the relationship between humanity and God, but also the relationships we hold with one another. The grace that is given is not meant to stop with us—it is meant to flow through us.

This is one of the clearest and most challenging implications of the gospel: those who have been forgiven are called to forgive.

The Foundational Call

Scripture makes this call unmistakably clear, instructing believers to be kind, tenderhearted, and forgiving toward one another, just as they themselves have been forgiven. This is not a suggestion or an optional expression of spiritual maturity; it is foundational. To receive forgiveness from God is to be drawn into a way of life that reflects that same mercy.

And yet, this is often where the struggle begins. It is one thing to accept forgiveness when we are aware of our own need, but it is another thing entirely to extend it when we have been deeply wronged.

The Inconsistency of the Heart

Jesus addressed this tension directly through the story of the servant who was forgiven an unpayable debt. Though his massive debt was erased, he immediately demanded payment from someone who owed him a much smaller amount.

- **The Exposure:** This story reveals the inconsistency of receiving grace for ourselves while demanding justice for others.
- **The Transformation:** To truly understand forgiveness is to be changed by it. It is not simply an act, but evidence of an inward transformation.
- **The New Perspective:** Grasping God's forgiveness reshapes how we see others, acknowledging their wrong without holding it as a debt to be repaid.

Releasing the Right to Revenge

To forgive is not to excuse, to forget, or to pretend harm did not occur. Rather, it is the decision to:

- **Release the right to revenge.**
- **Let go of the need to settle the score.**
- **Entrust justice to God** rather than carrying it ourselves.

Breaking the Cycle

Unforgiveness has a way of binding a person to the offense, keeping the wound active and the past continually influencing the present. It breeds resentment and fuels anger.

"Forgiveness breaks that cycle. It does not erase the memory, but it removes its control."

It creates space for healing, peace, and freedom. In choosing to forgive, believers reflect the mercy they have received and bear witness to a way of living that stands out in a world marked by retaliation and division.

This process may not happen instantly, but it remains essential—not because the offense was small, but because the mercy we received was great.

14: The Struggle to Forgive

Forgiveness, when received, can feel freeing. Forgiveness, when required, can feel impossible. There is a difference between understanding forgiveness and living it out. While we are aware of our own need for grace, extending that same grace to someone who has caused real pain brings us face to face with the deepest struggles of the human heart.

The Internal Resistance

When a wound runs deep, forgiveness does not feel like a simple choice—it feels like a battle. Several things within us resist the act of letting go:

- **Pride:** It refuses to humble itself before the offender.
- **Pain:** The fresh memory of the wound demands acknowledgement.
- **The Desire for Justice:** We want wrong to be accounted for, and we fear that releasing the offense diminishes its seriousness.

Even the apostle Peter wrestled with this, seeking a limit or a boundary to how much he was required to endure. Yet, the response remains the same: our forgiveness must reflect the boundless grace we ourselves have received.

The Danger of Holding On

Holding on to an offense can feel like control or protection, but what we hold on to does not remain neutral. Unforgiveness, left unaddressed, begins to take root and grow into bitterness.

- **Bitterness Relives the Pain:** It keeps the wound open and the past present.
- **Bitterness Shapes the Heart:** It changes how a person thinks, feels, and relates to others.
- **Bitterness Imprisons:** Instead of protecting the heart, it anchors the individual to a past they cannot change.

"Forgiveness does not erase the past, but it removes its control. It does not undo what was done, but it changes how it is carried."

Reframing the Memory

A common misunderstanding is that forgiveness requires "forgetting" or amnesia. Scripture does not teach this; rather, it teaches us to *remember differently*.

Consider the example of Joseph:

- **He remembered clearly:** He did not forget what his brothers had done to him .
- **He reframed history:** He chose to see the event through the lens of God's providence rather than personal pain .

- **He released revenge:** He acknowledged the harm without allowing it to define his identity or dictate his future.

A Spiritual Enablement

This level of forgiveness is not natural; it is spiritual. It is not produced by human effort, but by the grace of God working within the heart. We are not asked to produce something we have not first received—forgiveness flows from the grace that already takes root in us.

15: When Forgiveness Feels Impossible

There are moments when forgiveness does not feel difficult—it feels impossible. This is not because the command is unclear, but because the wound has reached into places that were once safe: trust, identity, and security. When harm is significant, the idea of forgiving can feel overwhelming, unfair, and even wrong.

The Protection of Holding On

In these moments, holding on can feel like a form of protection. It feels like the only way to:

- **Honor what happened:** ensuring the wrong is not minimized or dismissed.
- **Maintain Control:** preventing the offense from going "unanswered".
- **Ensure Justice:** fearing that forgiveness erases the weight of the act.

Defining Forgiveness Correctly

To move forward, we must clarify what forgiveness is *not*.

- It is *not* the denial of pain.
- It is *not* the approval of wrongdoing.
- It is *not* the removal of necessary boundaries.

"Forgiveness does not say, 'It was okay.' It says, 'I will not carry this any longer.'"

Willingness Over Feeling

Forgiveness does not begin with a surge of positive emotion; it begins with a quiet decision of the will . Sometimes it starts with a simple, honest prayer: *"I am not ready, but I do not want to stay here"*.

Because forgiveness is a process, God meets us in the struggle. He does not rush the healing or dismiss the depth of the wound. He walks with us through the tension and hesitation, providing the grace needed to release the debt.

The Bondage of Unforgiveness

We must face the reality that what we hold onto does not remain inactive. Unforgiveness, while it feels protective, often becomes a form of bondage. It keeps the pain alive and allows the past to dictate the future.

- **Forgiveness loosens the grip:** It creates space for restoration that cannot occur while the offense is being held.
- **Forgiveness is for freedom:** It is given because the heart was never meant to carry that weight indefinitely.

Hope in the Reach of God

Even in the most difficult situations and the deepest wounds, there remains hope. What feels impossible for us is not impossible for God. He is able to heal what has been deeply wounded and lead us, step by step, into a place we could not reach on our own. In that journey, the wound no longer defines the person, and the past no longer determines the future.

The Patience of the Process

One of the greatest comforts in the face of impossible forgiveness is that God does not demand an immediate or perfect emotional resolution. He is not a distant observer waiting for us to "get it right" before He helps us; He meets us in the middle of the mess.

- **He meets us in the tension:** Between the desire to obey and the reality of the pain.
- **He meets us in the hesitation:** When we take one step forward and two steps back.
- **He meets us in the silence:** When the hurt is too deep for words.

God does not rush the healing. Instead, He walks faithfully beside us, providing the grace not only to be forgiven but eventually, to extend that forgiveness to others.

Trusting the Higher Judge

When we cannot find the strength to forgive, it is often because we are trying to be the final judge of the situation. We can find relief by shifting that burden:

- **Entrusting the Outcome:** We must trust the God who sees fully and judges rightly.
- **Releasing the Weight:** We can let go of the need for an earthly resolution, knowing that God's justice is complete.
- **Resting in His Strength:** We are not producing this mercy on our own; it is His grace working through us.

A New Reality

Over time, the intensity of the pain begins to soften. The memory remains, but it loses its sharp edge and its authority over our future. We begin to see that what Christ has done for us is truly greater than what anyone has done *to* us.

This is where the unthinkable becomes possible. It is not a forced change, but one that is formed through divine grace, leading us to a place of peace and restoration we could never have reached alone.

Because what is impossible for us—

is never beyond the reach of God.

16: Healing & Transformation

Divine forgiveness does not end at pardon—it begins there. It reaches far beyond the legal removal of guilt and moves into the hidden places of the human heart where shame has settled and regret has taken root. Forgiveness does not simply address what has been done; it transforms who a person believes themselves to be.

The Verdict of No Condemnation

For many, the deepest struggle is not whether God *can* forgive, but whether they can live as if they *have been* forgiven. The memory of failure lingers, and the voice of condemnation remains persistent. However, Scripture speaks a final word over the believer:

"There is no condemnation for those who are in Christ Jesus."

This is not a suggestion or a reduced sentence; it is a final verdict. It means the accusations that once held weight no longer have authority. While the past is remembered, the record has been cleared.

The Process of Internal Healing

Transformation begins as forgiveness confronts the lies, we have believed for years. It interrupts the cycle of self-condemnation and introduces a grace that is given rather than earned. As this grace is received, the impact extends beyond the spiritual into the emotional and psychological:

- **The Weight Lifts:** The constant pressure to prove oneself begins to dissolve.
- **The Mind Quiets:** Patterns of anxiety, fear, and inner conflict lose their hold.
- **Instability is Replaced:** Assurance and rest take the place of striving and fear.

Forgiveness addresses the "root" of the issue, restoring dignity where there was once disgrace.

Outward Transformation

A healed heart does not remain closed—it opens. Those who have truly received forgiveness begin to reflect it in their daily lives. They become:

- **Less Guarded:** No longer defined by past wounds.
- **More Gracious:** Extending grace where they once withheld it.
- **More Empathetic:** Creating space for trust and understanding in their communities.

Movement Toward Purpose

Forgiveness does not produce passivity; it produces movement. Restoration produces a unique kind of humility and a willingness to meet others where they are without judgment.

The apostle Paul stands as the ultimate example of this: his past did not disqualify him; it became the backdrop against which grace was displayed. True forgiveness changes more than where a person stands—it changes who they become.

17: Shame, Identity and the Lies We Believe

Forgiveness may be received in a moment, but identity is often restored over time. There is a profound difference between being forgiven and believing that you are forgiven. One is a reality secured by God; the other is a truth that must be learned, embraced, and lived in.

In the space between these two realities, many find themselves struggling with how they see themselves in the light of grace.

The Persistent Voice of Shame

Even after forgiveness, shame can remain persistently in our thoughts and reactions. It shows up as hesitation, self-doubt, and an inability to fully receive love.

- **The Core Message:** Guilt says, "I made a mistake," but shame says, "I am the mistake".
- **The Narrative Shift:** Shame attaches itself to who we are, not just what we have done.
- **The False Definition:** It convinces us that our past is our definition and that we must carry labels never intended for us.

Confronting the Lies

Shame thrives on lies that shape our behavior and how we approach God. Some are loud, like *"I have gone too far,"* while others are subtle, like *"I have to prove that I've changed"*.

These lies keep a person bound to a place they have already been released from. For many, shame feels more "justified" or "honest" than grace, but it is not the truth.

"If sin has been dealt with, then its power to define has been removed. If the record has been cleared, then the labels attached to it no longer hold authority."

The Renewal of the Mind

Transformation involves the renewal of the mind—learning to see and think differently. It requires replacing familiar lies with unchanging truths:

- **You are not what you have done**.
- **You are not what was done to you**.
- **You are not defined by your worst moment**.

If you have been forgiven, you have been made new—not partially, but completely. This shift does not happen automatically; it is practiced and chosen by giving God's voice more authority than the voice of shame.

Anchored in Grace

Slowly, as the truth is embraced, the need to hide fades. In its place comes a grounding security not built on performance or perfection, but anchored in grace.
When identity is no longer shaped by shame, it is free to be shaped by truth. This truth does not change with circumstance or weaken with failure because it is based entirely on what Christ has done. It is this truth that allows a person to finally live as who they were truly made to be.

The Battle of the Voices

The restoration of identity is often a struggle between two competing narratives. On one side is the voice of the Accuser, which uses the memory of past sin to argue that forgiveness is a legal fiction—that underneath the "pardon," you are still the same broken person. On the other side is the voice of Truth, which declares that the old has passed away and the new has come.

- **Shame's Strategy:** It waits for moments of weakness or new failures to resurface, attempting to reclaim ground it no longer owns.
- **The Goal of the Lie:** It seeks to keep the believer at a distance from God, convinced that they are a "probationary" child rather than a fully accepted one.
- **The Power of Truth:** Truth does not argue with the past; it simply removes its authority.

Reclaiming the "Quiet Assumptions"

Much of the work in this stage of healing involves dragging "quiet assumptions" into the light. These are the subtle ways we self-sabotage because we don't believe we deserve the life grace has provided.

"Shame convinces us to carry what has already been lifted. It silences the truth with something that feels more familiar, because for many, shame feels more believable than grace."

To break this cycle, a person must intentionally:

- **Question the Hesitation:** Ask why there is a struggle to receive love or why rejection is always anticipated.
- **Reject the Labels:** Consciously choose to stop identifying as "the addict," "the failure," or "the person who went too far".
- **Practice the Truth:** Return to the reality of the Cross as a daily exercise until the voice of God becomes more familiar than the voice of the past.

Security Beyond Performance

Ultimately, the goal of this chapter is to move the reader toward a grounded security. This security is unique because it is not maintained by the believer's perfection, but by Christ's finished work.

When the struggle is no longer about *securing* acceptance, it becomes about *growing* in the freedom that has already been given. Identity is finally settled—not in what we have done, but in who we have been made to be.

18: Forgiveness & Eternal Life

Forgiveness is not simply a comforting idea or a helpful aspect of the Christian life; it is essential. It serves as the dividing line between death and life, and between distance from God and eternal communion with Him.

The Essential Barrier

Throughout Scripture, the story of humanity is marked by estrangement—a real barrier created by sin that no human effort can remove.

- **The Consequence:** Sin separates, corrupts, and leads to death.
- **The Limitation:** No amount of morality or intention can bridge the gap because the problem is too deep.
- **The Solution:** Forgiveness is what restores access and makes reconciliation possible.

Without this restoration, the prospect of eternal life is not simply uncertain—it is unattainable.

The Foundation of Salvation

The message of the gospel presents forgiveness not as an addition to salvation, but as its very foundation. To receive forgiveness is to be made alive again and restored to the One from whom we were separated.

"The resurrection declares that death has been overcome, that sin no longer has the final word, and that the life offered through Christ is not temporary—it is eternal."

The Rhythm of Relationship

While forgiveness secures our future, it also shapes our present through a living, active relationship. This is where *confession* becomes essential—not to earn forgiveness again, but to maintain the relationship.

- **Honesty:** Confession is about returning and remaining aware of sustaining grace.
- **Alignment:** We are not reentering forgiveness; we are learning to live within it.
- **Humility:** This ongoing rhythm keeps the heart soft and prevents spiritual complacency.

The Promise of Full Restoration

Ultimately, forgiveness points forward to a day when every trace of brokenness will be removed. Scripture promises a reality where:

- **Sorrow and pain** will no longer exist.
- **Full restoration** will replace reconciliation in part.
- **Eternal communion** with God will be the final state of peace and wholeness.

Forgiveness is the doorway into this promised reality. It is the assurance that what has been restored will never be lost again, securing a future that is life with God, forever.

19: Living as the Forgiven

Forgiveness changes more than a person's standing before God—it reshapes how they move through the world. It alters the lens through which life is interpreted, reorienting what holds ultimate weight. To live as the forgiven is to live as though what has happened in the past no longer has the authority it once did.

A Life of Awareness, Not Perfection

This way of living is not marked by perfection, but by a growing awareness that identity is anchored in something already secured.

- **Redefining Failure:** Failure is no longer final.
- **Recognizing Remnants:** Weakness is seen as a remnant of what has been overcome, rather than a defining characteristic.
- **The Work of Memory:** The goal is not to earn forgiveness again, but to remember it accurately and stand in it.

From Proving to Resting

Living as the forgiven moves a person from self-reliance to dependence.

- **Removing Pressure:** It removes the pressure to establish worth through actions.

- **Motivated by Alignment:** Obedience is no longer driven by fear or the need to secure acceptance; it is an expression of it.
- **The Freedom to be Honest:** It creates the freedom to acknowledge weakness without a total collapse of self, because identity is not self-constructed.

Relational Grace

When a person is no longer trying to secure their own worth, they become less transactional with others.

- **Reduced Defensiveness:** There is less need to control, prove, or defend.
- **Natural Mercy:** The capacity to extend mercy increases as a reflection of what has been received.
- **Clarity in Conflict:** Sin is addressed from a place of clarity rather than fear, and confession becomes a simple act of returning.

"Living as the forgiven is not about building a life in order to be accepted; it is living a life because acceptance has already been given."

Resilient Movement

Forgiveness provides an anchor that holds even when circumstances feel uncertain. It prevents pain from becoming ultimate and moves the believer outward into the world.

Life becomes less about self-preservation and more about participation in something larger than oneself. This is seen in ordinary choices:

- **Responding** rather than reacting.
- **Listening** rather than defending.
- **Consistency** and quiet faithfulness.

Over time, this way of living becomes a natural expression as the truth takes root and the identity becomes settled.

20: The Invitation

Forgiveness is not a small idea. It is not a side note in the Christian faith, nor is it a concept reserved for the spiritually mature. Forgiveness is the very heart of the gospel—the place where everything changes.

Without it, humanity remains trapped—bound to sin, burdened by guilt, and separated from God. No amount of effort, morality, or self-improvement can repair what sin has broken. Left to ourselves, we remain trying to fix what we cannot fix and carrying what we were never meant to carry.

The Way Provided

But God did not leave humanity in that condition. He did not stand at a distance, waiting for us to find our way back. Instead, He stepped into the very brokenness that separated us from Him.

Through Jesus Christ, God made a way where there was none.

- **A Deliberate Act:** The cross was an act of divine love.
- **A Full Payment:** Every sin and failure was paid for in full.
- **A Costly Grace:** Forgiveness was purchased with blood, yet it is offered freely .

A Complete Reorientation

Forgiveness is the moment a person is brought back into fellowship with the God who created them . It is the beginning of a new life and a complete reorientation of identity.

The forgiven are:

- **No longer defined by their past.**
- **No longer bound by what they have done.**
- **No longer carrying the weight of condemnation.**

This newness reaches the deepest parts of the soul, breaking the power of shame and healing what was once fractured.

The Personal Response

Forgiveness calls for a response. It requires us to lay down pride, release control, and surrender the need to justify ourselves. It also calls us to extend that same grace to others—a struggle that is made possible only through the mercy we ourselves have received.

Ultimately, this is about eternity. Through forgiveness, the door to eternal life is opened. What begins as reconciliation now will one day become complete restoration, where every wound is healed and every tear is wiped away.

The Standing Invitation

The question is not whether forgiveness is available—it is. The question is whether it will be received. This is where the message becomes personal.

"You do not need to clean yourself up first. You do not need to fix your life before you come. You only need to come. Come as you are."

Trust that what Christ has done is completely enough. If you have already received it, then live in it. Release the guilt that no longer belongs to you, let go of the shame that has been removed, and forgive as you have been forgiven.
Forgiveness is not just the beginning of the Christian life—it is the way we live it. It is the foundation we stand on and the promise that carries us all the way home.

The Scandal of the Finished Work

The world operates on the grueling treadmill of "more." More effort, more morality, more penance. We are taught that if we break something, we must be the ones to glue it back together. But the gospel shatters this logic. It declares that the distance created by sin was so vast that no human bridge could ever span it.

God did not wait for us to start the repair. He did not wait for us to prove we were sorry enough or "good enough" to be noticed. While we were still trapped in the brokenness, He stepped in.

- **It is not a negotiation:** God isn't checking your track record before offering the Cross.
- **It is not a probation:** You aren't being forgiven "on the condition" that you never trip again.
- **It is an accomplished fact:** Every hidden failure and every loud rebellion was accounted for and paid in full.

The Ultimate Exchange

At the Cross, a divine exchange took place. Christ took the identity we earned—the sinner, the failure, the separated—and gave us the identity He earned: the beloved, the righteous, the restored.

This is the beauty of the invitation. You aren't invited to a workshop on how to fix yourself. You are invited to a feast that has already been prepared. You are invited to a home where the door has already been unlocked.

The Final Move

If you are exhausted from trying to be "enough," let this be the moment you stop. If you are carrying a weight that was never yours to bear, let this be the moment you drop it. Forgiveness is not a goal to be reached; it is the ground you stand on.

You don't have to find your way back to God. Through Jesus Christ, God has already found His way back to you. The debt is canceled. The record is clear. The Father is waiting.

Stop striving. Just come home.

A Final Step Toward Grace

The truth of God's forgiveness is not merely meant to be understood—it is meant to be experienced. If you are weary from carrying the weight of the past or exhausted by the effort of trying to earn your way back to the Father, know that the door is already open. The "Ultimate Exchange" is available to you right now. Let these words be the start of your journey home.

A Prayer of Forgiveness

Heavenly Father,
I thank You for the profound truth that Your forgiveness is not a distant concept, but a finished reality secured through the precious blood of Your Son, Jesus Christ. I acknowledge before You that I cannot bridge the gap created by my own sin and that I am weary from the weight of trying to be "enough" on my own.
Right now, I choose to step out of the shadows of shame and into the light of Your unconditional love. I receive the "Ultimate Exchange"—releasing my failures to the Cross and embracing the new identity of a beloved, righteous, and restored child of God.
Thank You for finding me when I was lost. Grant me the grace to live every day as one who is truly forgiven, walking in the freedom and peace that only Your mercy can provide. I stop my striving today, and I finally come home to You.
In Jesus' name, Amen.

About the Author

Wazer H. Walker is a pastor, founder, visionary, and shepherd with a profound call to ministry that has spanned over three decades. Born into a large family in the community of Grove Place, Manchester, Jamaica, he was called by Jesus Christ in 1986. His formative years were marked by a tireless work ethic and five years of intense theological studies and internship. He was licensed in the United Church in Jamaica and the Cayman Islands in January 1991 and later ordained in September 1999 to the full-time ministry of the Word and Sacraments.

Driven by an intellectual curiosity and a deep desire to handle the Word of God with precision, Bishop Walker earned a Diploma in Theology from The Institute for Theological and Leadership Development (now The International University of the Caribbean) in Kingston, Jamaica. He firmly believes that higher theological education is more vital than secular education and that a servant of God should never stop learning. This commitment to excellence led him to earn a Bachelor of Arts and a Master of Arts in Biblical Studies, followed by a Master of Theology in Systematic Theology from Trinity College of the Bible and Theological Seminary in Indiana, USA. He was conferred with a Doctor of Divinity by Kingdom Builders Bible College and is currently a final-year candidate pursuing a Doctor of Theology (Th.D.).

In 2006, following the direction of the Lord, he established Echoes of Praise Ministries International Inc. (EOPM) in West Palm Beach, Florida. What began in his living room has grown into an international body dedicated to "plundering hell and populating heaven." His vision expanded further in 2017 with the birth of the Serious Gospel Communication Network, reaching souls globally through social and mainstream media. A certified International Chaplain and exceptional Christian counselor, Dr. Walker is known for a "hold no bars" preaching style that is both candid and full of spiritual insight.

Above all his professional achievements, Wazer H. Walker is a quintessential family man. He has been happily married to his wife, Elect Lady Minister Karen Walker, for 31 years. Together, they have been blessed with two children, Joel and Ruth-Ann.

www.ingramcontent.com/pod-product-compliance
Lightning Source LLC
LaVergne TN
LVHW040223110826
845146LV00004B/1268

* 9 7 9 8 9 9 5 5 9 4 7 4 1 *